STEP-BY-STEP

Pasta Dishes

Pasta Dishes

PAMELA WESTLAND

SHOOTING STAR PRESS

This edition printed in 1995 for:
Shooting Star Press Inc
230 Fifth Avenue – Suite 1212
New York, NY 10001

Shooting Star Press books are available at special discounts for bulk purchases for sales promotions, premiums, fund-raising, or educational use. Special edition or book excerpts can also be created to specification. For details contact: Special Sales Director, Shooting Star Press Inc., 230 Fifth Avenue, Suite 1212, New York, NY 10001

ISBN 1 56924 187 2

Printed in Italy

Acknowledgements:

Design & DTP: Pedro & Frances Prá-Lopez / Kingfisher Design
Art Direction: Lisa Tai
Managing Editor: Alexa Stace
Special Photography: Amanda Heywood
Home Economist: Carol Hanslip
Stylist: Marian Price

Gas Hob supplied by New World Domestic Appliances Ltd
Photographs on pages 6, 20, 40 & 60: By courtesy of ZEFA

Contents

First Courses

Pasta dishes perfectly fulfil the requirements of an opening course – to give family and friends an immediate feeling of well-being; to delight the eye, and excite but not dull the palate.

This is the time to serve clear but hearty soups contrasting the colors, textures and flavors of crisp, fresh vegetables and short pasta shapes; for a burst of mingled flavors such as those of roasted vegetables or spicy sausage, and for subtle, creamy sauces with herbs and nuts.

Serve the first course in the prettiest dishes you have, in scallop shells, or on glass plates. Serve hot dishes piping hot, cold ones refreshingly, tinglingly cold. Garnish each one with a leaf or a sprig or two of herbs, and serve them with a choice of breads in the Mediterranean style: long, crisp grissini breadsticks, olive ciabatta bread or warm baguettes.

Opposite: *An Italian fisherman and his wife inspect the nets. A wide variety of fish and shellfish are caught in the seas around the Italian coast, and this abundance is reflected in the antipasto dishes, which often include fish soups and seafood salads.*

STEP 1

STEP 2

STEP 3

STEP 4

HARICOT BEAN & PASTA SOUP

A dish with proud Mediterranean origins, this soup is a winter warmer, to be served with warm, crusty bread and, if you like, a slice of cheese.

SERVES 4

generous 1 cup dried haricot beans, soaked, drained and rinsed (see below)
4 tbsp olive oil
2 large onions, sliced
3 garlic cloves, chopped
1 x 15-oz can chopped tomatoes
1 tsp dried oregano
1 tsp tomato paste
3½ cups water
1 cup small pasta shapes, such as fusilli or conchigliette
½ cup sun-dried tomatoes, drained and thinly sliced
1 tbsp chopped cilantro, or flat-leaved parsley
2 tbsp grated Parmesan
salt and pepper

1 Put the soaked beans into a large saucepan, cover with cold water and bring them to the boil. Boil rapidly for 15 minutes, to remove any harmful toxins. Drain the beans in a colander.

2 Heat the oil in a saucepan over a medium heat and fry the onions until they are just beginning to change color. Stir in the garlic and cook for 1 further minute. Stir in the chopped tomatoes, oregano and the tomato paste and pour on the water. Add the beans, bring to the boil and cover the pot. Simmer for 45 minutes, or until the beans are almost tender.

3 Add the pasta, season the soup and stir in the sun-dried tomatoes. Return the soup to the boil, partly cover the pot and continue cooking for 10 minutes, or until the pasta is nearly tender.

4 Stir in the chopped herb. Taste the soup and adjust the seasoning if necessary. Transfer to a warmed soup tureen to serve, sprinkled with the cheese. Serve hot.

DRIED BEANS

You can soak the dried beans for several hours or overnight in a large bowl of cold water. Or, if it is more convenient, place them in a pot of cold water and bring them to the boil. Remove the pot from the heat and leave the beans to cool in the water. Drain and rinse the beans before beginning the recipe.

STEP 2

STEP 3

STEP 4

STEP 5

CHICKEN SCALLOPS

Served in scallop shells, this makes a stylish presentation for a dinner-party first course.

SERVES 4

2 cups short-cut macaroni, or other short
  pasta shapes
3 tbsp vegetable oil, plus extra for brushing
1 medium onion, finely chopped
3 pieces unsmoked Canadian bacon, chopped
2 cups button mushrooms, thinly sliced or
  chopped
¾ cup cooked chicken, diced
¾ cup crème fraîche
4 tbsp dry breadcrumbs
½ cup Cheddar cheese, grated
salt and pepper
flat-leaved parsley sprigs, to garnish

1 Cook the pasta in a large saucepan of boiling salted water to which you have added 1 tablespoon of the oil. When the pasta is almost tender, drain in a colander, return to the pot and cover.

2 Heat the broiler to medium. Heat the remaining oil in a skillet over medium heat and fry the onion until it is translucent. Add the chopped bacon and mushrooms and cook for a further 3-4 minutes, stirring once or twice.

3 Stir in the pasta, chicken and crème fraîche and season.

4 Brush 4 large scallop shells with oil. Spoon in the chicken mixture and smooth to make neat mounds.

5 Mix together the breadcrumbs and cheese and sprinkle over the top of the shells. Press the topping lightly into the chicken mixture, and broil for 4-5 minutes, until golden brown and bubbling. Garnish with parsley, and serve hot.

ALTERNATIVE

If you do not have scallop shells, you can assemble this dish in four small ovenproof dishes, such as ramekin dishes, or in one large one.

STEP 1

STEP 2

STEP 3

STEP 4

SPICY SAUSAGE SALAD

A warm sausage and pasta dressing spooned over chilled salad leaves makes a refreshing combination to start a meal.

SERVES 4

1 1/3 *cups small pasta shapes, such as elbow tubetti*
3 *tbsp olive oil*
1 *medium onion, chopped*
2 *cloves garlic, crushed*
1 *small yellow bell pepper, cored, seeded and cut into matchstick strips*
1 3/4 *cups spicy pork sausage such as chorizo, skinned and sliced*
2 *tbsp red wine*
1 *tbsp red wine vinegar*
mixed salad leaves, chilled
salt

1 Cook the pasta in a large saucepan of boiling salted water, adding 1 tablespoon of the oil. When it is almost tender, drain it in a colander and set aside.

2 Heat the remaining oil in a saucepan over a medium heat. Fry the onion until it is translucent, then stir in the garlic, bell pepper and sliced sausage and cook for 3-4 minutes, stirring once or twice.

3 Add the wine, wine vinegar and reserved pasta to the pot, stir to blend well and bring the mixture just to the boil.

4 Arrange the chilled salad leaves on 4 individual serving plates and spoon on the warm sausage and pasta mixture. Serve at once.

SPICED SAUSAGES

Chorizo is a Spanish spiced sausage. Another Spanish sausage to try is merguez, usually very hot. Other sausages to use are the Italian pepperoni, flavored with chili peppers, fennel and spices, and one of the many varieties of salami, usually flavored with garlic and pepper.

SPAGHETTI WITH RICOTTA CHEESE

This makes a quick and easy first course, ideal for the summer.

STEP 1

STEP 2a

STEP 2b

STEP 3

SERVES 4

12 oz spaghetti
3 tbsp olive oil
3 tbsp butter, cut into small pieces
2 tbsp chopped parsley

SAUCE:
1 cup freshly ground almonds
$^1/_2$ cup ricotta
large pinch of grated nutmeg
large pinch of ground cinnamon
$^2/_3$ cup crème fraîche
$^1/_2$ cup hot chicken stock
freshly ground black pepper
1 tbsp pine nuts
cilantro leaves, to garnish

1 Cook the spaghetti in a large saucepan of boiling salted water to which you have added 1 tablespoon of the oil. When it is almost tender, drain the pasta in a colander. Return to the pot and toss with the butter and parsley. Cover the pot and keep warm.

2 To make the sauce, mix together the ground almonds, ricotta, nutmeg, cinnamon, and crème fraîche to make a thick paste. Gradually pour on the remaining oil, stirring constantly until it is well blended. Gradually pour on the hot stock, stirring all the time, until the sauce is smooth.

3 Transfer the spaghetti to a warmed serving dish, pour on the sauce and toss well. Sprinkle each serving with pine nuts and garnish with cilantro leaves. Serve warm.

TOSSING SPAGHETTI

To toss spaghetti and coat it thoroughly with a sauce or dressing, use the 2 largest forks you can find – special forks are sold in some stores just for this purpose. Holding one fork in each hand, ease the prongs under the spaghetti from each side and lift them towards the center. Repeat evenly and rhythmically until the pasta is well and truly tossed.

STEP 2a

STEP 2b

STEP 2c

STEP 3

CHILLED NOODLES & PEPPERS

This is a convenient dish to serve when you are arriving home just before family or friends. You can have it all prepared and ready to assemble in minutes.

SERVES 4-6

½ lb ribbon noodles, or Chinese egg noodles
1 tbsp sesame oil
1 red bell pepper
1 yellow bell pepper
1 green bell pepper
6 scallions, cut into matchstick strips
salt

DRESSING:
5 tbsp sesame oil
2 tbsp light soy sauce
1 tbsp tahini (sesame paste)
4-5 drops hot pepper sauce

1 Preheat the broiler to medium. Cook the noodles in a large saucepan of boiling, salted water until they are almost tender. Drain them in a colander, run cold water through them, and drain thoroughly. Tip the noodles into a bowl, stir in the sesame oil, cover, and chill.

2 Cook the bell peppers under the broiler, turning them frequently, until they are blackened on all sides. Plunge into cold water, then skin them. Cut in half, remove the core and seeds and cut the flesh into thick strips. Set aside in a covered container.

To make the dressing, mix together the sesame oil, soy sauce, tahini and hot pepper sauce.

3 Pour the dressing on the noodles, reserving 1 tablespoon, and toss well. Turn the noodles into a serving dish, arrange the bell peppers over the noodles and spoon on the reserved dressing. Scatter on the scallion strips.

ALTERNATIVE

If you have time, another way of skinning peppers is to first broil them, then place in a plastic bag, seal and leave for about 20 minutes. The skin will then peel off easily.

16

VEGETABLE & PASTA SALAD

*Roasted vegetables and pasta make a delicious, colorful salad,
ideal as a first course or to serve with a platter of cold meats.*

STEP 1

SERVES 4
OVEN: 450°F

2 small eggplant, thinly sliced
1 large onion, sliced
2 large beefsteak tomatoes, skinned and cut
    into wedges
1 red bell pepper, cored, seeded and sliced
1 fennel bulb, thinly sliced
2 garlic cloves, sliced
4 tbsp olive oil
2 cups small pasta shapes, such as stars
1/2 cup feta cheese, crumbled
a few basil leaves, torn
salt and pepper
salad leaves, to serve

DRESSING:
5 tbsp olive oil
juice of 1 orange
1 tsp grated orange rind
1/4 tsp paprika
4 canned anchovies, finely chopped
pepper

1 Place the sliced eggplant in a colander, sprinkle with salt and set them aside for about 1 hour to draw out some of the bitter juices. Rinse under cold, running water to remove the salt, then drain. Toss on paper towels to dry.

2 Arrange the eggplant, onion, tomatoes, red bell pepper, fennel, and garlic in a single layer in an ovenproof dish, sprinkle on 3 tablespoons of the olive oil and season with salt and pepper. Bake in the preheated oven, uncovered, for 45 minutes, until the vegetables begin to turn brown. Remove from the oven and set aside to cool.

3 Cook the pasta in a large saucepan of boiling salted water to which you have added the remaining olive oil. When the pasta is almost tender, drain it in a colander, then transfer to a bowl.

4 To make the dressing, mix together the olive oil, orange juice, orange rind, and paprika. Stir in the anchovies and season with pepper. Pour the dressing over the pasta while it is still hot, and toss well. Set the pasta aside to cool.

5 To assemble the salad, line a shallow serving dish with the salad leaves and arrange the cold roasted vegetables in the center. Spoon the pasta in a ring around the vegetables and the feta cheese and basil leaves on top. Serve at once.

STEP 2

STEP 3

STEP 4

CHAPTER TWO

Pasta with Meat Sauces

Some of the most popular and widely known pasta dishes are ones
that bring together long strands of pasta cooked *al dente*,
and a rich, hearty sauce including beef or lamb,
chicken or ham. Spaghetti with meat sauce needs no introduction,
and yet it is said that there are almost as many versions of this
delicious Bolognese dish as there are lovers of Italian food. Our
version includes both beef and bacon in a sauce enriched
with beef stock and red wine.

Layered pasta dishes that are served in slices, wedges or squares are
perfect standbys for parties and picnics, buffet meals or informal
family occasions; children and teenagers love them.
Our selection includes creamy lasagne and Greek pasticcio,
eggplant and pasta cake, and an unusual meatloaf
with a contrasting pasta layer; they will all make
worthy additions to your repertoire
of baked pasta favorites.

Opposite: *Verdant landscape near Bologna, home of some splendid hams, as well as one of the best-known pasta sauces – Bolognese.*

SPAGHETTI CARBONARA

*Have all the cooked ingredients as hot as possible, so that the beaten
eggs are cooked on contact. It is a classic dish,
and one to serve with a flourish.*

STEP 1

SERVES 4

14 oz spaghetti
2 tbsp olive oil
1 large onion, thinly sliced'
2 garlic cloves, chopped
8 pieces bacon, cut into thin strips
2 tbsp butter
3 cups mushrooms, thinly sliced
1¼ cups heavy cream
3 eggs, beaten
¾ cup grated Parmesan, plus extra to serve,
*   optional*
freshly ground black pepper
sprigs of sage, to garnish

1 Heat a large serving dish or bowl.
Cook the spaghetti in a large
saucepan of boiling salted water, adding
1 tablespoon of the oil. When the pasta is
almost tender, drain in a colander.
Return the spaghetti to the pot, cover
and leave it in a warm place.

2 While the spaghetti is cooking,
heat the remaining oil in a skillet
over a medium heat. Fry the onion until
it is translucent, then add the garlic and
bacon and fry until the bacon
is crisp.

3 Remove the onion, garlic ,and
bacon with a slotted spoon and set
it aside to keep warm. Heat the butter in
the skillet and fry the mushrooms for 3-4
minutes, stirring them once or twice.
Return the bacon mixture to the
mushrooms. Cover and keep warm.

4 Stir together the cream, the beaten
eggs and cheese, and season with
salt and pepper.

5 Working very quickly to avoid
cooling the cooked ingredients, tip
the spaghetti into the bacon and
mushroom mixture and pour on the
eggs. Toss the spaghetti quickly, using 2
forks, and serve it at once. You can, if
you wish, hand around more grated
Parmesan cheese.

STEP 3

STEP 4

ACCOMPANIMENTS

A chilled salad of mixed leaves such as
young spinach, radicchio and endive
tossed in a vinaigrette dressing makes a
good accompaniment. You may also like
to serve a bowl of chilled radishes.

STEP 5

SPAGHETTI BOLOGNESE

This familiar meat sauce, known as ragu, may also be used in lasagne, and in other baked dishes. It is so versatile that it is a good idea to make it in large quantities, and freeze some.

STEP 1

STEP 2

STEP 3

STEP 4

SERVES 4

14 oz spaghetti
1 tbsp olive oil
salt
1 tbsp butter
2 tbsp chopped parsley, to garnish

RAGU SAUCE:
3 tbsp olive oil
3 tbsp butter
2 large onions, chopped
4 celery stalks, thinly sliced
8 pieces bacon, chopped
2 garlic cloves, chopped
1 lb lean ground beef
2 tbsp tomato paste
1 tbsp flour
1 x 15-oz can chopped tomatoes
$2/3$ cup beef stock
$2/3$ cup red wine
2 tsp dried oregano
$1/2$ tsp grated nutmeg
salt and pepper

1 To make the Ragu Sauce: heat the oil and the butter in a large skillet over a medium heat. Add the onions, celery and bacon and fry them for 5 minutes, stirring once or twice.

2 Stir in the garlic and ground beef and cook, stirring, until the meat has lost its redness. Lower the heat and continue to cook for an additional 10 minutes, stirring once or twice.

3 Increase the heat to medium, stir in the tomato paste and the flour and cook for 1-2 minutes. Stir in the chopped tomatoes, the beef stock, and wine and bring to the boil, stirring. Season the sauce and stir in the oregano and nutmeg. Cover the pot and simmer for 45 minutes, stirring occasionally.

4 Cook the spaghetti in a large saucepan of boiling salted water, adding the olive oil. When it is almost tender, drain in a colander, then return to the pot. Dot the spaghetti with the butter and toss thoroughly.

5 Taste the sauce and adjust the seasoning if necessary. Pour the sauce over the spaghetti and toss well. Sprinkle on the parsley to garnish and serve immediately.

STEP 1

STEP 2

STEP 4

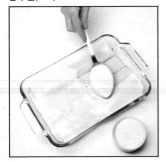

STEP 5

STUFFED CANNELONI

Cannelloni, the thick round pasta tubes, make perfect containers for close-textured sauces of all kinds.

SERVES 4
OVEN: 375°F

8 cannelloni tubes
1 tbsp olive oil
fresh herbs, to garnish

FILLING:
2 tbsp butter
10 oz frozen spinach, defrosted and chopped
¹/₂ cup ricotta
¹/₄ cup grated Parmesan
¹/₄ cup chopped ham
¹/₄ tsp grated nutmeg
2 tbsp heavy cream
2 eggs, lightly beaten
salt and pepper

SAUCE:
2 tbsp butter
¹/₄ cup flour
1¹/₄ cups milk
2 bay leaves
large pinch of grated nutmeg
¹/₄ cup grated Parmesan

1 To prepare the filling, melt the butter in a saucepan and stir in the spinach. Stir for 2-3 minutes to allow the moisture to evaporate, then remove the pot from the heat. Stir in the cheeses and the ham. Season with nutmeg, salt and pepper and beat in the cream and eggs to make a thick paste. Set aside to cool.

2 Cook the cannelloni in a large saucepan of boiling salted water, adding the olive oil. When almost tender, after 10-12 minutes, drain in a colander and set aside to cool.

3 To make the sauce, melt the butter in a saucepan, stir in the flour and cook for 1-2 minutes. Gradually pour on the milk, stirring all the time. Add the bay leaves, bring to simmering point, and cook for 5 minutes. Season with nutmeg, salt and pepper. Remove the pot from the heat and discard the bay leaves.

4 To assemble the dish, spoon the filling into a pastry bag and pipe it into each of the cannelloni tubes.

5 Spoon a little of the sauce into a shallow baking dish. Arrange the cannelloni in a single layer, then pour the remaining sauce on top. Sprinkle on the remaining Parmesan cheese and bake in the preheated oven for 40-45 minutes, until the sauce is golden brown and bubbling. Serve garnished with fresh herb sprigs.

LASAGNE VERDE

*The sauce in this delicious baked pasta dish is the same sauce
that is served with Spaghetti Bolognese (page 24).*

Serves 6
Oven 375°F

Ragù Sauce (see page 24)
1 tbsp olive oil
8 oz lasagne verde
½ cup Parmesan, grated
Bechamel sauce (see page 78)
salt and pepper
*green salad, tomato salad or black olives, to
    serve*

1 Begin by making the Ragù Sauce
as described on page 24. Cook the
sauce for 10-12 minutes longer than the
time given, in an uncovered skillet, to
allow the excess liquid to evaporate. To
layer the sauce with lasagne, it needs to
be reduced in this way until it has the
consistency of a thick paste.

2 Have ready a large saucepan of
boiling, salted water and add the
olive oil. Drop the pasta sheets into the
boiling water 2 or 3 at a time, and return
the water to the boil before adding
further sheets. If you are using fresh
lasagne, cook the sheets for a total of 8
minutes. If you are using dried or partly
precooked pasta, cook it according to the
directions on the package.

3 Spread a large, dampened dish
towel on the working surface. Lift
out the pasta sheets with a slotted spoon
and spread them in a single layer on the
towel. Use a second towel if necessary.
Set the pasta aside while you make the
Bechamel sauce, as described on page 78.

4 Grease a rectangular ovenproof
dish, about 10-11 in long. To
assemble the dish, spoon a little of the
meat sauce into the prepared dish, cover
with a layer of lasagne, then spoon over a
small amount of the Bechamel sauce and
sprinkle on a little cheese. Continue
making layers in this way, covering the
final layer of lasagne with the remaining
Bechamel sauce.

5 Sprinkle on the remaining cheese
and bake in the preheated oven for
40 minutes, until the sauce is golden
brown and bubbling. Serve with a chilled
green salad, a tomato salad, or a bowl of
black olives.

TAGLIATELLE WITH CHICKEN

Spinach ribbon noodles covered with a rich tomato sauce and topped with creamy chicken makes a very appetizing dish.

STEP 1a

STEP 1b

STEP 2

STEP 3

SERVES 4

¹/₂ lb fresh green ribbon noodles
1 tbsp olive oil
salt
basil leaves, to garnish
Tomato Sauce (see page 77)

CHICKEN SAUCE:
¹/₄ cup sweet butter
14 oz boned, skinned chicken breast,
    thinly sliced
³/₄ cup blanched almonds
1¹/₄ cups heavy cream
salt and pepper
basil leaves, to garnish

1 Make the Tomato Sauce as described on page 77, and keep warm.

2 To make the Chicken Sauce, melt the butter in a saucepan over a medium heat and fry the chicken strips and almonds for 5-6 minutes, stirring frequently, until the chicken is cooked through.

3 Meanwhile, pour the cream into a small saucepan over a low heat, bring it to the boil, and boil for about 10 minutes, until reduced by almost half.

Pour the cream over the chicken and almonds, stir well, and season. Set it aside and keep it warm.

4 Cook the fresh pasta in a large saucepan of boiling salted water, first adding the oil. When the pasta is just tender, about 5 minutes, drain in a colander, then return it to the pot, cover and keep it warm.

5 To assemble the dish, turn the pasta into a warmed serving dish and spoon the tomato sauce over it. Spoon the chicken and cream over the center, scatter the basil leaves over, and serve at once.

TOMATO SAUCE

This tomato sauce (see recipe on page 77) can be served with a variety of pasta dishes. Make double quantities and keep some in the freezer as a useful standby for quick and easy pasta meals.

STEP 2

STEP 5a

STEP 5b

STEP 6

LAYERED MEATLOAF

The cheesy pasta layer comes as a pleasant surprise inside this lightly spiced meatloaf.

SERVES 6
OVEN: 350°F

2 tbsp butter, plus extra for greasing
1 onion, finely chopped
1 small red bell pepper, cored, seeded and
  chopped
1 garlic clove, chopped
1 lb lean ground beef
½ cup soft white breadcrumbs
½ tsp cayenne pepper
1 tbsp lemon juice
½ tsp grated lemon rind
2 tbsp chopped parsley
4 bay leaves
8 slices bacon
1 cup short pasta, such as fusilli
1 tbsp olive oil
Cheese Sauce (see page 78)
salt and pepper
salad leaves, to garnish

1 Melt the butter in a skillet over a medium heat and fry the onion and pepper for about 3 minutes, until the onion is translucent. Stir in the garlic and cook it for a further 1 minute.

2 Put the meat into a large bowl and mash it with a wooden spoon until it becomes a sticky paste. Tip in the fried vegetables and stir in the breadcrumbs, cayenne, lemon juice, lemon rind and parsley. Season the mixture with salt and pepper and set it aside.

3 Cook the pasta in a large saucepan of boiling water to which you have added salt and the olive oil. When it is almost tender, drain in a colander.

4 Make the Cheese Sauce (see page 78). Stir in the pasta.

5 Grease a 2-lb loaf pan and arrange the bay leaves in the base. Stretch the bacon slices with the back of a knife blade and arrange them to line the base and the sides of the pan. Spoon in half the meat mixture, level the surface, and cover it with the pasta. Spoon in the remaining meat mixture, level the top, and cover the pan with foil.

6 Cook the meatloaf in the preheated oven for 1 hour, or until the juices run clear and the loaf has shrunk away from the sides of the pan. Pour off any excess fat and turn the loaf out on a warmed serving dish, loosening the edges if necessary. Serve hot, with a green salad.

STEP 2

STEP 3

STEP 5

STEP 6

EGGPLANT CAKE

Layers of toasty-brown eggplant, meat sauce and cheese-flavored pasta make this a popular family supper dish.

SERVES 4
OVEN: 375°F

1 medium eggplant, thinly sliced
5 tbsp olive oil
Lamb Sauce (see page 79)
2¹/₃ cups short pasta shapes, such as fusilli
¹/₄ cup butter, plus extra for greasing
6 tbsp flour
1¹/₄ cups milk
²/₃ cup light cream
²/₃ cup chicken stock
large pinch of grated nutmeg
³/₄ cup Cheddar cheese, grated
¹/₄ cup Parmesan, grated
artichoke heart and tomato salad, to serve

1 Put the eggplant slices in a colander, sprinkle with salt and leave for about 45 minutes, while the salt draws out some of the bitter juices. Rinse the eggplant under cold, running water and drain. Toss them in paper towels to dry.

2 Heat 4 tablespoons of the oil in a skillet over a medium heat. Fry the eggplant slices for about 4 minutes on each side, until they are light golden brown. Remove with a slotted spoon and drain on paper towels.

3 Make the Lamb Sauce as described on page 79 and keep warm.

4 Meanwhile, cook the pasta in a large saucepan of boiling salted water, adding 1 tablespoon of olive oil. When the pasta is almost tender, drain it in a colander and return it to the pot. Cover and keep warm.

5 Melt the butter in a small saucepan, stir in the flour and cook for 1 minute. Gradually pour on the milk, stirring all the time, then stir in the cream and chicken stock. Season with nutmeg, salt and pepper, bring to the boil and simmer for 5 minutes. Stir in the Cheddar cheese and remove from the heat. Pour half the sauce over the pasta and mix well. Reserve the remaining sauce.

6 Grease a shallow ovenproof dish. Spoon in half the pasta, cover it with half the meat sauce and then with the eggplant in a single layer. Repeat the layers of pasta and meat sauce and spread the remaining cheese sauce over the top. Sprinkle on the Parmesan cheese. Bake in the preheated oven for 25 minutes, until the top is golden brown. Serve hot or cold, with artichoke heart and tomato salad.

PASTICCIO

A recipe that has both Italian and Greek origins, this dish may be served hot or cold, cut into thick, satisfying squares.

STEP 1

STEP 2

STEP 4

STEP 5

SERVES 6
OVEN: 375°F

2¹/₃ cups fusilli, or other short pasta shapes
1 tbsp olive oil
4 tbsp heavy cream
salt
rosemary sprigs, to garnish

SAUCE:
2 tbsp olive oil, plus extra for brushing
1 onion, thinly sliced
1 red bell pepper, cored, seeded and chopped
2 cloves garlic, chopped
1¹/₄ lb lean ground beef
15 oz can chopped tomatoes
¹/₂ cup dry white wine
2 tbsp chopped parsley
1 x 2-oz can anchovies, drained and chopped
salt and pepper

TOPPING:
1¹/₄ cups plain yogurt
3 eggs
pinch of nutmeg
¹/₂ cup Parmesan, grated

1 To make the sauce, heat the oil in a large skillet and fry the onion and bell pepper for 3 minutes. Stir in the garlic and cook for 1 minute more. Stir in the beef and cook, stirring frequently, until it has changed color.

2 Add the tomatoes and wine, stir well and bring to the boil. Simmer, uncovered, for 20 minutes, until the sauce is fairly thick. Stir in the parsley and anchovies and adjust the seasoning.

3 Cook the pasta in a large saucepan of boiling salted water, adding the oil. When it is almost tender, drain it in a colander, then transfer it to a bowl. Stir in the cream and set it aside.

4 To make the topping, beat together the yogurt and eggs, and season the mixture with nutmeg, salt and pepper. Stir in the cheese.

5 Brush a shallow baking dish with oil. Spoon in half the macaroni and cover with half of the meat sauce. Repeat these layers, spread the topping evenly over the dish and sprinkle on the cheese.

6 Bake in the preheated oven for 25 minutes, until the topping is golden brown and bubbling. Garnish with rosemary and serve with a selection of raw vegetable crudités.

TAGLIATELLI WITH MEATBALLS

There is an appetizing contrast of textures and flavors in this satisfying family dish.

STEP 1

STEP 2a

STEP 2b

STEP 3

SERVES 4

1 lb lean ground beef
1 cup soft white breadcrumbs
1 garlic clove, crushed
2 tbsp chopped parsley
1 tsp dried oregano
large pinch of grated nutmeg
$^1/_4$ tsp ground cilantro
$^1/_2$ cup Parmesan, grated
2-3 tbsp milk
flour, for dusting
4 tbsp olive oil
14 oz tagliatelli
2 tbsp butter, diced
salt
2 tbsp chopped parsley, to garnish

SAUCE:
3 tbsp olive oil
2 large onions, sliced
2 celery stalks, thinly sliced
2 garlic cloves, chopped
1 x 15-oz can chopped tomatoes
$^1/_2$ cup bottled sun-dried tomatoes, drained
   and chopped
2 tbsp tomato paste
1 tbsp moist dark brown sugar
$^2/_3$ cup white wine, or water
salt and pepper

green salad, to serve

1 To make the sauce, heat the oil in a skillet and fry the onion and celery until translucent. Add the garlic and cook for 1 minute. Stir in the tomatoes, tomato paste, sugar and wine, and season. Bring to the boil and simmer for 10 minutes.

2 Break up the meat in a bowl with a wooden spoon until it becomes a sticky paste. Stir in the breadcrumbs, garlic, herbs, and spices. Stir in the cheese and enough milk to make a firm paste. Flour your hands, take large spoonfuls of the mixture and shape it into 12 balls. Heat 3 tablespoons of the oil in a skillet and fry the meatballs for 5-6 minutes until browned.

3 Pour the tomato sauce over the meatballs. Lower the heat, cover the skillet and simmer for 30 minutes, turning once or twice. Add a little extra water if the sauce begins to dry.

4 Cook the pasta in a large saucepan of boiling salted water, adding the remaining oil. When almost tender, drain in a colander, then turn into a warmed serving dish, dot with the butter and toss with 2 forks. Spoon the meatballs and sauce over the pasta and sprinkle on the parsley. Serve with a green salad.

CHAPTER THREE

Pasta with Fish Sauces

Macaroni with mushrooms and shrimp or squid; wholewheat lasagne with smoked fish and shrimp; pasta shells with mussels; spaghetti with smoked salmon or with anchovies and tuna; vermicelli with clams – these are irresistible combinations that have a whiff of the sea and, in most cases, the flavor of the Mediterranean.

These dishes are as practical as they are delicious, all perfect choices for the busy cook who has to keep an eye on the clock. In general, since fish and seafood need only the briefest of cooking times, the sauce and the pasta can be ready together, perfectly cooked and perfectly timed just as the family is assembling or the guests are arriving.

Opposite: *Open-air restaurant beside Lake Garda. The many rivers and lakes in Italy are a rich source of fish and shellfish, which feature largely in pasta sauces.*

SPAGHETTI WITH SEAFOOD SAUCE

Frozen shelled shrimp from the freezer can become the star ingredient in this colorful and tasty dish.

STEP 2

SERVES 4

*2¼ cups short-cut spaghetti, or ½ lb long
    spaghetti broken into 6-in lengths
2 tbsp olive oil
1¼ cups chicken stock
1 tsp lemon juice
1 small cauliflower, cut into flowerets
2 medium carrots, thinly sliced
1⅓ cups snow peas, trimmed
¼ cup butter
1 onion, sliced
3 medium zucchini, thinly sliced
1 garlic clove, chopped
2 cups frozen shelled shrimp, defrosted
2 tbsp chopped parsley
¼ cup Parmesan, grated
salt and pepper
½ tsp paprika, to sprinkle
4 unshelled shrimp, to garnish (optional)*

STEP 3a

1 Cook the spaghetti in a large saucepan of boiling salted water, adding 1 tablespoon of the olive oil. When it is almost tender, drain in a colander. Return to the pot and stir in the remaining olive oil. Cover the pot and keep warm.

2 Bring the chicken stock and lemon juice to a boil in a saucepan over medium heat and cook the cauliflower and carrots for 3-4 minutes, until they are barely tender. Remove with a slotted spoon and set aside. Add the snow peas to the stock and cook for 3-4 minutes, until they begin to soften. Remove with a slotted spoon and add to the other vegetables. Reserve the stock for future use.

3 Melt half the butter in a skillet over medium heat and fry the onion and zucchini for about 3 minutes. Add the garlic and shrimp and cook for a further 2-3 minutes, until they are thoroughly heated through.

4 Stir in the reserved vegetables and season well. When the vegetables are heated through stir in the remaining butter.

5 Transfer the spaghetti to a warmed serving dish. Pour on the sauce and parsley and toss well, using 2 forks, until thoroughly coated. Sprinkle on the grated cheese and paprika and garnish with unshelled shrimp, if using. Serve immediately.

STEP 3b

STEP 4

STEP 2

STEP 3

STEP 4a

STEP 4b

MACARONI & SHRIMP BAKE

This adaptation of an 18th-century Italian dish is baked until it is golden brown and sizzling, then cut into wedges, like a cake.

SERVES 4
OVEN: 350°F

3½ cups short pasta, such as short-cut
macaroni
1 tbsp olive oil, plus extra for brushing
6 tbsp butter, plus extra for greasing
2 small fennel bulbs, thinly sliced, leaves
reserved
3 cups mushrooms, thinly sliced
1 cup shelled shrimp
½ cup Parmesan, grated
2 large tomatoes, sliced
1 tsp dried oregano
salt and pepper
Bechamel Sauce (see page 78)
pinch of cayenne

1 Cook the pasta in a large saucepan of boiling, salted water to which you have added 1 tablespoon of olive oil. When the pasta is almost tender, drain it in a colander, return it to the pot and dot with 2 tablespoons of the butter. Shake the pot well, cover, and keep the pasta warm.

2 Melt the remaining butter in a skillet over medium heat and fry the fennel for 3-4 minutes, until it begins to soften. Stir in the mushrooms and fry for a further 2 minutes. Stir in the shrimp, remove the pot from the heat and set it aside.

3 Make the Bechamel Sauce and add the cayenne. Remove the pot from the heat and stir in the reserved vegetables, shrimp and the pasta.

4 Grease a round, shallow baking dish. Pour in the pasta mixture and spread evenly. Sprinkle on the Parmesan, and arrange the tomato slices in a ring around the edge of the dish. Brush the tomato with olive oil and sprinkle on the dried oregano.

5 Bake in the preheated oven for 25 minutes, until the top is golden brown. Serve hot.

ACCOMPANIMENT

A mixed green salad, tossed with the reserved fennel leaves and sprinkled with crumbled feta cheese, goes well with this dish.

SEAFOOD LASAGNE

*Layers of cheese sauce, smoked cod and wholewheat lasagne can be
assembled overnight and left ready to cook on the following day.*

STEP 2

SERVES 6
OVEN: 375°F

8 sheets wholewheat lasagne
1 lb smoked cod or other white fish
2½ cups milk
1 tbsp lemon juice
8 peppercorns
2 bay leaves
a few stalks of parsley
½ cup Cheddar, grated
¼ cup Parmesan, grated
salt and pepper
a few whole shrimp, to garnish (optional)

SAUCE:
¼ cup butter, plus extra for greasing
1 large onion, sliced
1 bell pepper, cored, seeded, and chopped
1 small zucchini, sliced
½ cup flour
⅔ cup white wine
⅔ cup light cream
¾ cup shelled shrimp
½ cup Cheddar, grated

1 Cook the lasagne in boiling, salted water until almost tender, as described on page 29. Drain and reserve.

2 Place the smoked fish, milk, lemon juice, peppercorns, bay leaves and parsley in a skillet. Bring to the boil, cover, and simmer for 10 minutes.

3 Remove the fish, skin and remove any bones. Flake the fish. Strain and reserve the liquor.

4 Make the sauce: melt the butter in a saucepan and fry the onion, bell pepper and zucchini for 2-3 minutes. Stir in the flour and cook for 1 minute. Gradually add the fish liquor, then stir in the wine, cream, and shrimp. Simmer for 2 minutes. Remove from the heat, add the cheese, and season.

5 Grease a shallow baking dish. Pour in a quarter of the sauce and spread evenly over the base. Cover the sauce with 3 sheets of lasagne, then with another quarter of the sauce. Arrange the fish on top, then cover with half the remaining sauce. Finish with the remaining lasagne, then the rest of the sauce. Sprinkle the Cheddar and Parmesan over the sauce.

6 Bake in the preheated oven for 25 minutes, or until the top is golden brown and bubbling. Garnish with a few whole shrimp, if liked.

STEP 4

STEP 5a

STEP 5b

PASTA SHELLS WITH MUSSELS

*Serve this aromatic seafood dish to family and friends
who admit to a love of garlic!*

STEP 1

STEP 2

STEP 3

STEP 5

SERVES 4-6

4 cups pasta shells
1 tbsp olive oil

SAUCE:
7¹/₂ pints mussels, scrubbed
2 large onions, chopped
1 cup dry white wine
¹/₂ cup sweet butter
6 large garlic cloves, finely chopped
5 tbsp chopped parsley
1¹/₄ cups heavy cream
salt and pepper
crusty bread, to serve

1 Pull off the "beards" from the mussels and rinse well in several changes of water. Discard any mussels that refuse to close when tapped. Put the mussels in a large saucepan with one of the onions and the white wine. Cover the saucepan, shake, and cook over a medium heat for 2-3 minutes until the mussels open.

2 Remove the pot from the heat, lift out the mussels with a slotted spoon, reserving the liquor, and set aside until they are cool enough to handle. Discard any mussels that have not opened.

3 Melt the butter in a saucepan over medium heat and fry the remaining onion until translucent. Stir in the garlic and cook for 1 further minute. Gradually pour on the reserved cooking liquor, stirring to blend thoroughly. Stir in the parsley and cream, season, and bring to simmering point. Taste and adjust the seasoning if necessary.

4 Cook the pasta in a large saucepan of salted boiling water, adding the oil. When it is almost tender, drain in a colander. Return the pasta to the pot, cover, and keep warm.

5 Remove the mussels from their shells, reserving a few for garnish. Stir the mussels into the cream sauce. Tip the pasta into a warmed serving dish, pour on the sauce and, using 2 large spoons, toss it well. Garnish with a few mussel shells. Serve hot, with warm, crusty bread.

PASTA SHELLS

Pasta shells, from medium-sized to giant ones, are ideal for this dish, because the rich, buttery sauce collects in the cavities and impregnates the pasta with the flavors of the shellfish and wine.

STEP 1

STEP 2

STEP 3a

STEP 3b

SPAGHETTI WITH SMOKED SALMON

Made in moments, this is a dish to astonish and delight unexpected guests.

SERVES 4

1 lb buckwheat spaghetti
2 tbsp olive oil
1/2 cup feta cheese, crumbled

SAUCE:
1 1/4 cups heavy cream
2/3 cup whisky or brandy
4 oz smoked salmon
large pinch of cayenne pepper
2 tbsp chopped cilantro, or parsley
salt and pepper

1 Cook the spaghetti in a large saucepan of salted boiling water, adding 1 tablespoon of the olive oil. When the pasta is almost tender, drain it in a colander. Return to the pot and sprinkle on the remaining oil. Cover and shake the pot and keep warm.

2 In separate small saucepans, heat the cream and the whiskey or brandy to simmering point, but do not let them boil.

3 Combine the cream and whiskey or brandy. Cut the smoked salmon into thin strips and add to the cream.

Season with pepper and cayenne, and stir in the chopped herb.

4 Transfer the spaghetti to a warmed serving dish, pour on the sauce and toss thoroughly using 2 large forks. Scatter the crumbled cheese over the pasta and garnish with cilantro leaves. Serve at once.

ACCOMPANIMENTS

A green salad with a lemony dressing is a good accompaniment to this rich and luxurious dish.

VERMICELLI WITH CLAM SAUCE

Another cook-in-a-hurry recipe that transforms cupboard ingredients into a dish with style.

STEP 1

SERVES 4

14 oz vermicelli, spaghetti, or other long
  pasta
1 tbsp olive oil
2 tbsp butter
2 tbsp flaked Parmesan, to garnish
sprig of basil, to garnish

SAUCE:
1 tbsp olive oil
2 onions, chopped
2 garlic cloves, chopped
2 x 7-oz jars clams in brine
½ cup white wine
4 tbsp chopped parsley
½ tsp dried oregano
pinch of grated nutmeg
salt and pepper

1 Cook the pasta in a large saucepan of boiling salted water, adding the olive oil. When it is almost tender, drain in a colander, return to the pot and add the butter. Cover the pot. Shake it and keep it warm.

2 To make the clam sauce, heat the oil in a saucepan over a medium heat and fry the onion until it is translucent. Stir in the garlic and cook for 1 further minute.

3 Strain the liquid from one jar of clams, pour into the pot and add the wine. Stir well, bring to simmering point and simmer for 3 minutes. Drain the brine from the second jar of clams and discard. Add the shellfish and herbs to the pot and season with pepper and nutmeg. Lower the heat and cook until the sauce is heated through.

4 Transfer the pasta to a warmed serving dish, and pour on the sauce. Sprinkle on the Parmesan and garnish with the basil. Serve hot.

STEP 2

STEP 3a

PARMESAN

You could use grated Parmesan for this dish, but flakes of fresh Parmesan, carved off the block, will give it an added depth of flavor.

STEP 3b

SPAGHETTI WITH TUNA & PARSLEY

This is a recipe to look forward to when parsley is at its most prolific, in the growing season.

STEP 2a

STEP 2b

STEP 3a

STEP 3b

SERVES 4

1 lb spaghetti
1 tbsp olive oil
2 tbsp butter
black olives, to garnish

SAUCE:
1 x 7-oz can tuna, drained
1 x 2-oz can anchovies, drained
1 cup olive oil
1 cup roughly chopped parsley
2/3 cup crème fraîche
salt and pepper

1 Cook the spaghetti in a large saucepan of salted boiling water, adding the olive oil. When it is almost tender, drain in a colander and return to the pot. Add the butter, toss thoroughly to coat and keep warm.

2 Remove any bones from the tuna. Put it into a blender or food processor with the anchovies, olive oil, and parsley, and process until the sauce is smooth. Pour in the crème fraîche and process for a few seconds to blend. Taste the sauce and season

3 Warm 4 plates. Shake the pot of spaghetti over medium heat until it is thoroughly warmed through. Pour on the sauce and toss quickly, using 2 forks. Garnish with the olives and serve immediately with warm, crusty bread.

KNOW YOUR OIL

Oils produced by different countries, mainly Italy, Spain and Greece, have their own characteristic flavors. Some olive varieties produce an oil which has a hot and peppery taste, while others, such as the Kalamata, grown in Greece, give a distinctly "green" flavor. Get to know and recognize the different grades of oil, too. Extra virgin olive oil, the finest grade, is made from the first, cold pressing of olives. Virgin olive oil, which has a fine aroma and color, is also made by cold pressing. It may have a slightly higher acidity level than extra virgin oil. Refined or pure olive oil is made by treating the paste residue with heat or solvents to remove the residual oil. Olive oil is a blend of refined and virgin olive oil.

STEP 2

STEP 3a

STEP 3b

STEP 5

STEAMED PASTA & FISH

A tasty mixture of creamy fish and pasta cooked in a bowl, unmolded and drizzled with tomato sauce, presents macaroni in a new guise.

SERVES 4

generous 1 cup short-cut macaroni, or other
    short pasta shapes
1 tbsp olive oil
1 tbsp butter, plus extra for greasing
1 lb white fish fillets, such as cod or haddock
a few parsley stalks
6 black peppercorns
$1/2$ cup heavy cream
2 eggs, separated
2 tbsp chopped dill, or parsley
freshly ground black pepper
pinch of grated nutmeg
$1/2$ cup Parmesan, grated
Tomato Sauce (see page 77), to serve
dill or parsley sprigs, to garnish

1 Cook the pasta in a large saucepan of salted boiling water, adding the oil. Drain in a colander, return to the pot, add the butter and cover the pot. Keep the pasta warm.

2 Place the fish in a skillet with the parsley stalks and peppercorns and pour on just enough water to cover. Bring to the boil, cover, and simmer for 10 minutes. Lift out the fish with a fish slice, reserving the liquor. When the fish is cool enough to handle, skin and remove any remaining bones. Cut into bite-sized pieces.

3 Transfer the pasta to a large bowl and stir in the cream, egg yolks, and dill. Stir in the fish, taking care not to break it up, and enough liquor to make a moist but firm mixture. It should fall easily from a spoon but not be too runny. Whisk the egg whites until stiff but not dry, then fold into the mixture.

4 Grease a heatproof bowl and spoon in the mixture to within 1½ in of the rim. Cover the top with greased waxed paper and a cloth, or with foil, and tie firmly around the rim. Do not use foil if you cook the dish in a microwave.

5 Stand the bowl on a trivet in a large saucepan of boiling water to come halfway up the sides. Cover and steam for 1½ hours, topping up the boiling water as needed, or cook in a microwave on maximum power for 7 minutes.

6 Run a knife around the inside of the bowl and invert on to a warmed serving dish. Pour some tomato sauce over the top and serve the rest separately. Garnish with the herb sprigs.

SQUID & MACARONI STEW

This Greek dish is quick and easy to make, yet has all the authentic flavor of the islands.

STEP 2a

STEP 2b

STEP 3

STEP 4

SERVES 4-6

2¼ cups short-cut macaroni, or other short
   pasta shapes
1 tbsp olive oil
2 tbsp chopped parsley
salt and pepper

SAUCE:
12 oz cleaned squid
6 tbsp olive oil
2 onions, sliced
1 cup fish stock
²/₃ cup red wine
¾ lb tomatoes, skinned and thinly sliced
2 tbsp tomato paste
1 tsp dried oregano
2 bay leaves

1 Cook the pasta for only 3 minutes in a large saucepan of boiling salted water, adding the oil. When it is almost tender, drain the pasta in a colander, return to the pot, cover, and keep warm.

2 Cut the squid into 1½-in strips. Heat the oil in a saucepan over medium heat and fry the onion until translucent. Add the squid and stock and simmer for 5 minutes. Pour on the wine and add the tomatoes, tomato paste,

oregano and bay leaves. Bring the sauce to the boil, season, and cook, uncovered, for 5 minutes.

3 Add the pasta, stir well, cover the saucepan and continue simmering it for 10 minutes, or until the macaroni and squid are almost tender. By this time the sauce should be thick and syrupy. If it is too liquid, uncover the pot and continue cooking for a few minutes. Taste the sauce and adjust the seasoning if necessary.

4 Remove the bay leaves and stir in most of the parsley, reserving a little to garnish. Transfer to a warmed serving dish. Sprinkle on the remaining parsley and serve hot. Serve with warm, crusty bread such as ciabatta.

CLEANING SQUID

Peel off the skin and cut off the head and tentacles. Remove the transparent bone from the body, then turn the body sac inside out and wash thoroughly. Cut off the tentacles to use and discard the head.

CHAPTER FOUR

Pasta & Vegetable Dishes

Eggplant shells filled with mozzarella cheese and pasta shapes; crisp and crunchy vegetables like celery and bell peppers stir-fried with pasta shells and tossed in a sweet- and-sour sauce; a Spanish pasta omelet of just-cooked eggs flavored with onion, fennel and garlic – this section takes you on a gastronomic tour around the world.

Whether you choose to simmer vegetables lightly in water or stock, to steam them or to stir-fry them, be sure to cook them only until they, like the pasta, are *al dente* and still slightly crisp. In this way the vegetables will retain more of their nutrients and most of their color and will contrast both appealingly and deliciously with their pasta accompaniment.

Opposite: *The rolling hills of Val d'Oreia, near Pienza, Tuscany. Much of the country's food – grains, rice, meat, fruit and vegetables – is produced in the fertile Tuscan soil.*

PASTA WITH GREEN VEGETABLES

The different shapes and textures of the vegetables make a mouthwatering presentation in this light and summery dish.

STEP 2a

STEP 2b

STEP 4a

STEP 4b

SERVES 4

2¼ cups gemelli or other pasta shapes
1 tbsp olive oil
2 tbsp chopped parsley
salt and pepper

SAUCE:
1 head green broccoli, cut into flowerets
2 medium zucchini, sliced
½ lb asparagus spears, trimmed
1¼ cups snow peas, trimmed
1 cup frozen peas
2 tbsp butter
3 tbsp vegetable stock
5 tbsp heavy cream
large pinch of grated nutmeg
2 tbsp grated Parmesan

1 Cook the pasta in a large pot of salted boiling water, adding the olive oil. When almost tender, drain the pasta in a colander and return to the pot, cover and keep warm.

2 Steam the broccoli, zucchini, asparagus spears and snow peas over a saucepan of boiling, salted water until they are just beginning to soften. Remove from the heat and plunge into cold water to prevent them from cooking further in the residual heat. Drain and set them aside.

3 Cook the frozen peas in boiling, salted water for 3 minutes, then drain. Refresh in cold water and drain again.

4 Put the butter and vegetable stock in a saucepan over a medium heat. Add all the vegetables except the asparagus spears and toss carefully with a wooden spoon to heat through, taking care not to break them up. Stir in the cream, allow the sauce just to heat through and season well with salt, pepper and nutmeg.

5 Transfer the pasta to a warmed serving dish and stir in the chopped parsley. Spoon the sauce over, and sprinkle on the Parmesan. Arrange the asparagus spears in a pattern on top. Serve hot.

VEGETARIAN CASSOULET

A satisfying winter dish, this vegetable and pasta cassoulet is derived from the slow-cooked, one-pot meals of the Languedoc, in the south of France.

STEP 1

STEP 3

STEP 5a

STEP 5b

Serves 6
Oven: 350°F

generous 1 cup dried haricot beans, soaked and drained
2¼ cups penne, or other short pasta shapes
6 tbsp olive oil
3½ cups vegetable stock
2 large onions, sliced
2 cloves garlic, chopped
2 bay leaves
1 tsp dried oregano
1 tsp dried thyme
5 tbsp red wine
2 tbsp tomato paste
2 celery stalks, sliced
1 fennel bulb, sliced
2 cups mushrooms, sliced
½ lb tomatoes, sliced
salt and pepper
1 tsp moist dark brown sugar
4 tbsp dry white breadcrumbs
salad leaves and crusty bread, to serve

1 Put the beans in a large saucepan, cover them with water, and bring to the boil. Boil the beans rapidly for 20 minutes, then drain them.

2 Cook the pasta for only 3 minutes in a large saucepan of boiling salted water, adding 1 tablespoon of the oil. When almost tender, drain the pasta in a colander and set it aside.

3 Place the beans in a large flameproof casserole, pour on the vegetable stock and stir in the remaining olive oil, the onions, garlic, bay leaves, herbs, wine and tomato paste.

4 Bring the stock to the boil, cover the casserole and cook it in the oven for 2 hours.

5 Add the reserved pasta, the celery, fennel, mushrooms, and tomatoes, and season with salt and pepper. Stir in the sugar and sprinkle on the breadcrumbs. Cover the casserole and continue cooking it for 1 hour. Serve it hot, with salad leaves and plenty of crusty bread.

NOTE

Do not use a salted vegetable stock for the initial cooking stage of this dish, since the salt would inhibit the softening process of the beans as they gradually absorb the liquid.

STEP 2

STEP 3

STEP 4

STEP 6

VEGETABLE PASTA STIR-FRY

*Prepare all the vegetables and cook the pasta in advance,
then the dish can be cooked in a few minutes.*

SERVES 4

4 cups wholewheat pasta shells, or other
    short pasta shapes
1 tbsp olive oil
2 carrots, thinly sliced
16-18 baby sweetcorn
3 tbsp peanut oil
1 in ginger root, peeled and thinly sliced
1 large onion, thinly sliced
1 garlic clove, thinly sliced
3 celery stalks, thinly sliced
1 small red bell pepper, cored, seeded and
    sliced into matchstick strips
1 small green bell pepper, cored, seeded and
    sliced into matchstick strips
salt

SAUCE:
1 tsp cornstarch
2 tbsp water
3 tbsp soy sauce
3 tbsp dry sherry
1 tsp clear honey
few drops of hot pepper sauce (optional)

steamed snow peas, to serve

1 Cook the pasta in a large saucepan of boiling salted water, adding the olive oil. When almost tender, drain the pasta in a colander, return to the pot, cover and keep the pasta warm.

2 Cook the sliced carrot and baby sweetcorn in boiling, salted water for 2 minutes, then drain in a colander, plunge into cold water to prevent further cooking, and drain again.

3 Heat the peanut oil in a wok or a large skillet over medium heat and fry the ginger for 1 minute, to flavor the oil. Remove with a slotted spoon and discard.

4 Add the onion, garlic, celery and bell peppers to the oil and stir-fry for 2 minutes. Add the carrots and baby sweetcorn and stir-fry for a further 2 minutes, then stir in the reserved pasta.

5 Put the cornstarch into a small bowl and gradually pour on the water, stirring constantly. Stir in the soy sauce, sherry, and honey.

6 Pour the sauce into the saucepan, stir well and cook for 2 minutes, stirring once or twice. Taste the sauce and season with hot pepper sauce, if liked. Serve with a steamed green vegetable such as snow peas.

BAKED EGGPLANT WITH PASTA

Combined with tomatoes and Mozzarella cheese, pasta makes a
tasty filling for baked eggplant shells.

STEP 2

SERVES 4
OVEN: 400°F

2¼ *cups penne, or other short pasta shapes*
4 *tbsp olive oil, plus extra for brushing*
2 *medium eggplant*
1 *large onion, chopped*
2 *garlic cloves, crushed*
1 *x 15-oz can chopped tomatoes*
2 *tsp dried oregano*
2 *oz mozzarella cheese, thinly sliced*
¼ *cup Parmesan, grated*
2 *tbsp dry breadcrumbs*
salt and pepper

green salad, to serve

1 Cook the pasta in a large saucepan of salted boiling water, adding 1 tablespoon of the olive oil. When it is almost tender, drain the pasta in a colander, return to the pot, cover, and keep warm.

2 Cut the eggplant in half lengthwise. Score around the inside with a knife, then scoop out the flesh with a spoon, taking care not to pierce the skin. Brush the insides of the eggplant shells with olive oil. Chop the eggplant flesh and set it aside.

3 Heat the remaining oil in a skillet over a medium heat and fry the onion until it is translucent. Add the garlic and fry for 1 further minute. Add the chopped eggplant and fry for 5 minutes, stirring frequently. Add the tomatoes and oregano and season with salt and pepper. Bring to the boil and simmer for 10 minutes, or until the mixture is thick. Taste and adjust the seasoning if necessary. Remove from the heat and stir in the reserved pasta.

4 Brush a baking sheet with oil and arrange the eggplant shells in a single layer. Divide half the tomato mixture between the four shells. Arrange the mozzarella on top and cover with the remaining mixture, piling it into a mound. Mix together the Parmesan and breadcrumbs, and sprinkle over the top, patting it lightly into the mixture.

5 Bake in the preheated oven for 25 minutes, until the topping is golden brown. Serve hot, with a green salad.

STEP 3

STEP 4a

STEP 4b

STEP 2

STEP 3

STEP 4

STEP 5

VERMICELLI PIE

*Lightly cooked vermicelli is pressed into a pie pan and baked
with a creamy mushroom filling.*

SERVES 4
OVEN: 350°F

½ lb vermicelli or spaghetti
1 tbsp olive oil
2 tbsp butter, plus extra for greasing
salt

SAUCE:
¼ cup butter
1 onion, chopped
2¼ cups button mushrooms, trimmed
1 green bell pepper, cored, seeded and
 sliced into thin rings
⅔ cup milk
3 eggs, lightly beaten
2 tbsp heavy cream
1 tsp dried oregano
pinch of grated nutmeg
freshly ground black pepper
1 tbsp grated Parmesan

tomato and basil salad, to serve

1 Cook the pasta in a large saucepan of
salted boiling water, adding the olive
oil. When almost tender, drain in a colander.
Return to the pot, add the butter and shake
the pot well.

2 Grease a 8-in loose-bottomed pie pan.
Press the pasta on the base and round
the sides to form a case.

3 Heat the butter in a skillet over a
medium heat and fry the onion well
until it is translucent. Remove with a
slotted spoon and spread it in the pie case.

4 Add the mushrooms and bell pepper
rings to the skillet and turn them in
the fat until they are glazed. Fry them for
about 2 minutes on each side, then arrange
in the pie case.

5 Beat together the milk, eggs, and
cream, stir in the oregano, and season
with nutmeg and pepper. Pour the mixture
carefully over the vegetables and sprinkle
on the cheese.

6 Bake the pie in the preheated oven for
40-45 minutes, until filling is set.
Slide onto a serving plate and serve warm.

VARIATIONS

You can use this moist and buttery flan
case with any of your favorite fillings:
chopped bacon, cheese and herbs, or a
mixture of diced ham and sliced
mushrooms; or cooked and flaked smoked
haddock with corn kernels.

STEP 3a

STEP 3b

STEP 3c

STEP 4

SPANISH OMELET

Use any leftover cooked pasta you may have, such as penne, short-cut macaroni or shells, to make this fluffy omelet an instant success.

SERVES 2

4 tbsp olive oil
1 small Spanish onion, chopped
1 fennel bulb, thinly sliced
³/₄ cup raw potato, diced and dried
1 garlic clove, chopped
4 eggs
1 tbsp chopped parsley
pinch of cayenne pepper
scant ¹/₂ cup cooked short pasta
1 tbsp stuffed green olives, halved, plus extra
    to garnish
salt and pepper
marjoram sprigs, to garnish
tomato salad, to serve

1 Heat 2 tablespoons of the oil in a heavy skillet over a low heat and fry the onion, fennel, and potato for 8-10 minutes, stirring occasionally, until the potato is just tender. Do not allow it to break up. Stir in the garlic and cook for 1 further minute. Remove from the heat, lift out the vegetables with a slotted spoon, and set them aside. Rinse and dry the skillet.

2 Break the eggs into a bowl and beat them until they are frothy. Stir in the parsley, and season with salt, pepper, and cayenne.

3 Heat 1 tablespoon of the remaining oil in a saucepan over medium heat. Pour in half the beaten eggs, then add the cooked vegetables, the pasta, and the olives. Pour on the remaining egg and cook until the sides begin to set.

4 Lift up the edges with a spatula to allow the uncooked egg to spread underneath. Continue cooking the omelet, shaking the pot occasionally, until the underside is golden brown.

5 Slide the omelet out onto a large, flat plate and wipe the skillet clean with paper towels. Heat the remaining oil in the skillet and invert the omelet. Cook on the other side until it is also golden brown.

6 Slide the omelet on to a warmed serving dish. Garnish with a few olives and marjoram, and serve hot, cut into wedges, with a tomato salad.

GETTING TO KNOW PASTA

BASIC PASTA DOUGH

If you get caught up in the enthusiasm of pasta making, you might like to buy a machine to roll, stretch, and cut the dough. Once it is fully and evenly stretched, it is surprisingly easy to cut by hand.

SERVES 4

1 cup all-purpose flour, plus
    extra for dusting
2/3 cup fine semolina
1 tsp salt
2 tbsp olive oil
2 eggs
2-3 tbsp hot water

1. Sieve the flour, semolina, and salt into a bowl and make a well in the center. Pour in half the oil and add the eggs. Add 1 tablespoon of hot water and, using your fingertips, work to a smooth dough. Sprinkle on a little more water if necessary to make the dough pliable.

2. Lightly dust a board with flour, turn out the dough and knead it until it is elastic and silky. This might take 10-12 minutes. Dust the dough with more flour if your fingers become sticky.

Alternatively, put the eggs, 1 tablespoon hot water, and the oil in the bowl of a food processor and process for a few seconds.

continued opposite

Pasta means "paste" or "dough" in Italian, and many of the widely popular pasta dishes have their origins in Italy, where pasta has been produced at least as far back as the 13th century.

Its principal ingredients are modest, though more and more types of fresh and dried pasta are coming on to the market. By far the most widely available commercial type is made from hard durum wheat, milled to form fine semolina grains and then extruded through drums fitted with specially perforated disks. The production methods may not sound inspiring, but the end product certainly is. The wide variety of these disks makes it possible to produce an estimated 600 different pasta shapes and sizes, including strands and shells, twists and spirals, rings and tubes.

VARIETIES OF PASTA

You can choose pasta that is made from just the endosperm of the wheat, as most of it is, or from the whole wheat; this type contains more dietary fiber. Other basic types are made from ground buckwheat, which gives the product a grayish color and distinctively nutty flavor that combines especially well with vegetable and herb sauces; with the addition of spinach paste, which produces an attractive green color – *lasagne verde* is a popular example; and with a proportion of tomato paste, which produces a deep coral-like coloring. *Pasta all'uovo*, which is made with the addition of eggs, is

invariably produced in a range of flat shapes and those, too, are available in fresh and dried forms.

Colored Pasta

As well as green pasta, colored with spinach, and red pasta, made with tomato paste, there are other colors available: saffron pasta is an attractive yellow-orange color, beet-colored pasta is a deep pink, and pasta colored with squid ink is a dramatic black. You can also buy or make pasta flecked with chopped basil and other herbs.

THE PASTA FAMILY

Pasta is generally divided into three main categories, long and folded pasta, noodles, and short pasta, the group that offers, perhaps, the greatest scope for inspired presentation and recipe variation.

Since dried pasta has a shelf life of up to six months (see the panel on storage) and fresh pasta may be safely frozen for up to six months, it is a good idea to build up your own store of pasta selections to surprise and delight your family and friends.

Pasta Dictionary

The names of the various types and shapes of pasta have a romantic and evocative ring to them, conjuring up thoughts of warm, sunny climates and rich, herby sauces. But if you are not conversant with the similarities of tagliatelli and tagliarini, or the difference between cappelletti and conchiglie, you can find yourself longing for a translation. This glossary of some of the most popular pasta shapes should help you.

anelli and anellini rings small pasta used in soup

bozzoli deeply-ridged, cocoon-like shapes

bucatini long, medium-thick tubes

cappelletti wide-brimmed-hat shapes

cappelli d'angelo "angel's hair", thinner than cappellini

cappellini fine strands of ribbon pasta, usually sold curled into a nest shape

casareccia short curled lengths of pasta twisted at one end

cavatappi short, thick corkscrew shapes

conchiglie ridged shells

conchigliette little shells used in soup

cornetti ridged shells

cresti di gallo curved shapes, resembling cocks' combs

ditali, ditalini short tubes

eliche loose spiral shapes

elicoidali short, ridged tubes

farfalle butterflies

fedeli, fedelini fine tubes twisted into "skeins"

festonati short lengths, like garlands

fettuccine ribbon pasta, narrower than tagliatelle

fiochette, fiochelli small bow shapes

frezine broad, flat ribbons

fusilli spindles, or short spirals

fusilli bucati thin spirals, like springs

gemelli "twins", two pieces wrapped together

gramigna meaning "grass" or "weed"; the shapes look like sprouting seeds

lasagne flat, rectangular sheets

linguini long, flat ribbons

lumache smooth, snail-like shells

lumachine U-shaped flat noodles

macaroni, maccheroni long or short-cut tubes, may be ridged or elbow shapes

maltagliati triangular-shaped pieces, traditionally used in bean soups

noodles fine, medium, or broad flat ribbons

orecchiette dished shapes; the word means "ear"

orzi tiny pasta, like grains of rice, used in soups

pappardelle widest ribbons, either straight or sawtooth-edged

pearlini tiny disks

penne short, thick tubes with diagonal-cut ends

pipe rigate ridged, curved pipe shapes

rigatoni thick, ridged tubes

ruoti wheels

Basic Pasta Dough cont.

3. Add the flour, semolina and salt, and process until smooth. Sprinkle on a litle more hot water if necessary to make the dough pliable. You can then transfer the dough to an electric mixer and knead for 2-3 minutes, using the dough hook.

4. Divide the dough into 2 equal pieces. Cover a working surface with a clean cloth or dish towel and dust it liberally with flour. Place one portion of the dough on the floured cloth and roll it out as thinly and evenly as possible, stretching the dough gently until the pattern of the weave shows through. Cover it with a cloth and roll out the second piece in a similar way.

5. Cut the dough into shapes of your choice. Use a ruler and a sharp knife blade to cut long, thin strips for noodles, or small confectionery cutters to cut circles, stars, or other decorative shapes.

6. Cover the dough shapes with a clean cloth and leave them in a cool place, not the refrigerator, for 30-45 minutes to become partly dry. Or place them in an airtight container for up to 24 hours.

7. Cook the fresh pasta in a large saucepan of boiling salted water, adding 1 tablespoon olive oil, for 3-4 minutes, until almost tender. Drain the pasta in a colander and serve with the sauce of your choice.

SPINACH & RICOTTA RAVIOLI

Serves 4

1 recipe basic pasta dough (see above)
12 oz frozen spinach, thawed and chopped
¾ cup ricotta, or equal amounts each of full-fat cream cheese and cottage cheese to make ¾ cup
4 tbsp grated Parmesan
salt and pepper
large pinch grated nutmeg

For the Sauce
1 tbsp butter
⅔ cup crème fraîche
grated nutmeg

1. Turn the chopped spinach into a colander and use a wooden spoon to press out as much of the liquid as possible.

2. Mix together the spinach and cheeses, and season the mixture with salt, pepper, and nutmeg. (For a smooth filling, you can mix the ingredients in a food processor.)

3. Divide the dough into two equal pieces and roll out each one as described on page 75. Cut one sheet into strips about 3-in wide. Place small heaps of the filling at 3-in intervals close to one side of each strip. Fold the strips over, press the edges to seal them, and repeat with the remainder of the dough. Cut out the ravioli squares. A pastry wheel is useful for this, as it helps to seal the joins as it cuts.

continued opposite

semini seed shapes

spaghetti fine, medium or thick rods

spirale two rods twisted together into spirals

strozzapreti "priest strangler", double twisted strands

tagliarini flat, ribbon-like strips, thinner than tagliatelli

tagliatelli broad, flat ribbons

tortiglione thin, twisted tubes

vermicelli fine, slender strands usually sold folded into skeins

ziti tagliati short, thick tubes

Nutritional Value

Pasta has frequently had to answer to the charge that it is a fattening food to be avoided by anyone on a weight-reducing diet. The answer to that charge is that it may not be the pasta that piles on the calories, more likely some of the sauces we choose to serve with it.

This table will help you to sound out the dietary and nutritional credentials of dry pasta.

	per 100g
Average moisture content	11.10
Protein	13.20
Fat	2.80
Dietary fibre (approx.)	10.00
Starch (as monosaccharide)	65.70
Calories	327.00

Twisting and twirling

There is undoubtedly a knack to eating long spaghetti and other pasta strands. The timid may be tempted to cut the strands into short lengths and pick them up on a fork, but that is not the way the Italians do it.

You need a spoon and a fork; no knife. Hold the fork in your right hand (if you are right-handed) and use it to pick up a bundle of spaghetti strands. Hold the spoon in your other hand, rest the prongs of the fork against the center of the bowl and twirl the fork around, wrapping the spaghetti around it in a tight circle.

When there are no loose or dangling spaghetti strands, put the spoon down and convey the forkful of pasta deftly to your mouth. It is easy when you know how!

COOKING PASTA

The enjoyment of pasta depends on its being cooked to perfection; not too little, when it will be crisp and unyielding and taste of raw flour; not too much, when it will be too soft and the strands or shapes will probably stick together.

The Italians describe the perfect texture as *al dente*, meaning that the pasta is not quite tender, and still slightly resistant to the bite.

Cooking times vary according to the type and volume of the pasta, and you should always follow those recommended on the package. In general, fresh pasta will be cooked in 3-5 minutes. Dried pasta becomes *al dente* in around 6 minutes for fine strands such as vermicelli; 7-12 minutes for quick-cooking macaroni, for spaghetti and noodles; and 10-15 minutes for cannelloni tubes and sheets of lasagne.

Whatever the pasta type, have ready a large saucepan of water at a steady, rolling boil. Add salt, and 1 tablespoon of olive oil, which will prevent the pieces from sticking together. Add the pasta gradually, a handful or a few strands at a time so that the water continues to boil. Hold the spaghetti and other long strands in one hand, lower them into the water and, as the pasta softens, twist the top so that the strands wind around the base of the saucepan.

Keep the water at a gentle, rolling boil. This action will help to prevent the pasta from sticking. Do not completely cover the pot, or the water will boil over. Leave it uncovered, or partly cover it with a tilted lid.

Drain the cooked pasta into a colander and, if it is not to be served at once, return it to the saucepan with a little butter or olive oil.

How much to allow
Appetites and occasions vary, and it is not possible to say exactly how much pasta to allow for each guest.
It is worth remembering that dried pasta more than doubles in volume during cooking, absorbing water or other liquid until it is rehydrated.

It is usual to allow 1-2 oz, or ⅓-⅔ cup, dried pasta per person for a first course or a salad, and 3-4 oz, or 1-1¼ cups, dried pasta for a main dish.

Crispy pasta fries
If you are serving pasta as an accompaniment to a main dish, and you have some left over, you might like to serve it as a crisply fried snack.

Cut long strands such as spaghetti or macaroni into short lengths. Toss the pasta shapes with a fork to separate them.

Heat vegetable oil in a deep pot to moderately hot, 180°F, and drop in one piece of pasta. It should sizzle and turn brown within 30 seconds.

Fry the pasta in small batches, in a frying basket if you have one. If not, lift out the golden-brown pasta with a draining spoon, toss it on paper towels to dry, and fry the remainder in a similar way.

Use the pasta as croûtons, as a garnish for soups; to scatter over green salad, or as a snack with drinks.

Storing and freezing pasta
Dried pasta will keep in good condition for up to six months. Keep it in the package, and reseal it once you have opened it, or transfer the pasta to an airtight jar. You can buy tall glass spaghetti jars for long strands, and store other shapes decoratively in a row of tightly covered glass jars.

Fresh pasta has a short storage life, only one or two days in the refrigerator, so buy it only when you want to serve it, and follow the advice on the package.

Cooked pasta may be stored for up to three days in the refrigerator. If the pieces have stuck together, turn them in a colander and run warm water through them to separate them. Drain well, then toss the pasta in hot olive oil or melted butter before serving.

Freeze cooked pasta dishes in covered containers for up to 3 months. Thaw at room temperature before reheating.

Spinach & Ricotta Ravioli cont.
4. Cook the ravioli in a large pot of boiling water, to which you have added salt and 1 tbsp olive oil, for 3-4 minutes.

5. Heat together the butter and crème fraîche, and season the sauce with salt, pepper, and nutmeg.

6. Drain the pasta in a colander, turn it into a warmed serving dish and pour over the sauce. Toss the ravioli to coat it thoroughly.

TOMATO SAUCE

2 tbsp olive oil
1 small onion, chopped
1 garlic clove, chopped
1 x 15-oz can chopped tomatoes
2 tbsp chopped parsley
1 tsp dried oregano
2 bay leaves
2 tbsp tomato paste
1 tsp sugar

1. To make the tomato sauce, heat the oil in a saucepan over a medium heat and fry the onion until it is translucent. Add the garlic and fry for 1 further minute.

2. Stir in the chopped tomatoes, parsley, oregano, bay leaves, tomato paste, and sugar and bring the sauce to the boil.

3. Simmer, uncovered, until the sauce has reduced by half, about 15-20 minutes. Taste the sauce and adjust the seasoning if necessary. Discard the bay leaves.

BECHAMEL SAUCE

1¼ cups milk
2 bay leaves
3 cloves
1 small onion
¼ cup butter, plus extra for
    greasing
6 tbsp flour
1¼ cups light cream
large pinch of grated nutmeg
salt and pepper

1. Pour the milk into a small saucepan and add bay leaves. Press the cloves into the onion, add to the pot and bring the milk to the boil. Remove from the heat and set it aside to cool.

2. Strain the milk into a pitcher and rinse the saucepan. Melt the butter in the pot and stir in the flour. Stir for 1 minute, then gradually pour on the milk, stirring constantly. Cook the sauce for 3 minutes, then pour on the cream and bring it to the boil. Remove from the heat and season with nutmeg, salt and pepper.

CHEESE SAUCE

2 tbsp butter
1 tbsp flour
1 cup milk
2 tbsp light cream
pinch of grated nutmeg
⅓ cup Cheddar cheese, grated
1 tbsp grated Parmesan cheese

1. Melt the butter in a saucepan, stir in the flour and cook for 1 minute.

continued opposite

PASTA MACHINES

Pasta machines that will stretch and roll the dough are now widely available. You will need plenty of space for the rolled-out dough, as well as somewhere to hang the dough to dry, once it has been cut.

The correct technique is to feed the pasta through the rollers one notch at a time. This is time-consuming but important, as the pasta needs to be thinned gradually so that it keeps its elasticity.

To roll the pasta from the recipe on page 74, first divide the dough into 2 pieces. If the pasta strip becomes too long and unwieldy as it stretches, cut it again. Roll until all the pieces have gone through the machine at each setting, from the highest down to the thinnest. Lay out the pasta on dish towels to dry.

Leave the pasta to dry until it feels leathery before you attempt to cut it, though it must not be so dry that it is brittle. The machine will cut pasta into strips for ribbon pasta; other shapes will have to be cut by hand. To use pasta strips immediately, place a dish towel over the back of a chair and hang the strips there to dry. Traditionally, a broom handle was stretched across the room, and the pasta hung over it.

PASTA SAUCES

Getting to know the individual pasta shapes is one of the delights of this form of cookery, and creative cooks will enjoy partnering their favorite sauces with first one and then another type of pasta. Although there are classic combinations such as Spaghetti Bolognese, when the pasta is tossed with the rich meat and tomato sauce of southern Italy, and Spaghetti Carbonara, when the eggs in the sauce are cooked on contact with the piping hot pasta, there are no hard and fast rules, just guidelines.

These guidelines are largely a matter of practicality. Long, slender strands of pasta combine well with meat, fish, and vegetable sauces, without absorbing the liquid element or concealing the shape and texture of the principal ingredient. Twisted, curved, and hollow pasta shapes are ideal to serve with runny sauces, which get deliciously trapped in, say, the cavities of large pasta shells, and small shapes and fine strands are especially good for adding body and texture to clear meat, fish and vegetable soups.

Appearance is a factor in creating partnerships of pasta and sauce. Shells are an obvious example, to evoke the appropriate mental image when combined with fish and seafoods. Taste comes into the decision-making process too. It may seem improbable, but it is a fact that spaghetti tossed with a green vegetable sauce does taste different from, say, pasta wagon wheels served with the identical sauce. And a calamares stew would lose much of its robust character if it were made with tiny pasta stars instead of macaroni.

Cheeses with Pasta
Some cheeses have a natural affinity with pasta dishes and appear frequently in recipes. It is always worth having a supply in store, handy for use at short

notice. If you have difficulty in buying Parmesan in a whole piece, try a good Italian food store or delicatessen.

Ricotta A milky white, soft and crumbly Italian cheese which resembles cottage cheese. It is low in fat, being traditionally made from whey, but some varieties produced now have a proportion of whole milk added. If you cannot obtain ricotta, use another low-fat soft cheese, or cottage cheese. To obtain a smooth-textured sauce or filling, press cottage cheese through a sieve.

Parmesan A mature and exceptionally hard cheese produced in Italy. Parmesan, properly known as Parmigiano-reggiano, plays such an important part in the overall flavor of pasta dishes that it is worth exploiting its potential to the full. It may be useful to have a small carton of ready-grated Parmesan in the refrigerator, but you will find that it quickly loses its characteristic pungency and "bite". For that reason, it is better to buy small quantities of the cheese in one piece (it is usually very expensive) and grate it yourself as needed. Tightly wrapped in plastic wrap and foil, it will keep in the refrigerator for several months. Grate it just before serving, for maximum flavor. To grate a large quantity by hand is time-consuming, as the cheese is so hard: you may find it easier to use a food processor.

Pecorino A hard sheep's milk cheese which resembles Parmesan and is often used for grating over dishes. It has a sharp flavor and is only used in small quantities. Best bought in the piece and stored, tightly wrapped in plastic wrap and foil, in the refrigerator.

Mozzarella Another highly popular cheese, often found in pasta dishes. It is a soft, fresh cheese, with a piquant flavor, traditionally made from water buffalo's milk, and is usually sold surrounded by whey to keep it moist. Buffalo milk is now scarce, and so nowadays this cheese is often made with cow's milk. It can be used fresh, most popularly in tomato salads, and is also often added to provide a tangy, chewy layer to baked dishes.

OLIVE OIL

Olive oil, which is at the heart of so many pasta dishes, has a personality all of its own, and each variety has its own characteristic flavor. The main oil-producing countries are Italy, Greece and Spain. It is important to be able to recognize the different grades of oil.

Extra-virgin olive oil This is the finest grade, made from the first, cold pressing of hand gathered olives. Always use extra-virgin oil for salad dressings.

Virgin olive oil This oil has a fine aroma and color, and is also made by cold pressing. It may have a slightly higher acidity level than extra-virgin oil.

Refined or "pure" olive oil This is made by treating the paste residue from the pressings with heat or solvents to remove the residual oil.

Olive oil is a blend of refined and virgin olive oil.

Cheese Sauce cont.

2. Gradually pour on the milk, stirring all the time. Stir in the cream and season the sauce with nutmeg, salt and pepper.

3. Simmer the sauce for 5 minutes to reduce, then remove it from the heat and stir in the cheeses. Stir until the cheese has melted and blended into the sauce.

LAMB SAUCE

2 tbsp olive oil
1 large onion, sliced
2 celery stalks, thinly sliced
1 lb lean ground lamb
3 tbsp tomato paste
$^2/_3$ cup bottled sun-dried
  tomatoes, drained and chopped
1 tsp dried oregano
1 tbsp red wine vinegar
$^2/_3$ cup chicken stock
salt and pepper

1. Heat the oil in a skillet over a medium heat and fry the onion and celery until the onion is translucent. Add the lamb, stirring frequently, and fry until it changes color.

2. Stir in the tomato paste, sun-dried tomatoes, oregano, wine vinegar and stock, and season with salt and pepper.

3. Bring the sauce to the boil and cook, uncovered, for about 20 minutes until the meat has absorbed the stock. Taste the sauce and adjust the seasoning if necessary.

INDEX